The HOME GARDENER'S Journal

National Home Gardening Club

Welcome to *The Home Gardener's Journal*

Each year offers gardeners new gardening challenges, new plants, new equipment and new ways to tailor the garden. But how to keep track of it all? This Journal—published exclusively for National Home Gardening Club Members—is a valuable gardening tool you won't want to be without. Make a week-by-week record of gardening details on these pages, and the Journal will help you see the "big picture" of your garden. To keep a journal is to know the rhythms and pulse of your garden. Journaling will also help you solve a variety of garden challenges by giving you a detailed record of past events. Enjoy using this Journal, and enjoy your garden!

National Home Gardening Club

Contents

Using The Journal   4

Planning Your Garden   5
A Seasonal Gardening Calendar
Drawing a Garden Plan
Sample Garden Designs
My Garden's Profile
My Own Plans

Keeping Your Journal   17
Weekly Charts
Plant Profiles
Tips and Reminders

Planting Records 51
Seed-Starting Profiles
Transplanting and Harvest Notes

Gardening Resources 65
Contacts, Gardens, Clubs

References 69
Maps, Charts and Glossary

© 2011 National Home Gardening Club® • 12301 Whitewater Drive, Minnetonka, MN 55343 • ISBN: 978-1-58159-476-8 • 10 9 8 7 6 5 4

Using *The Home Gardener's Journal*

Some gardeners take a "seat-of-the-pants" approach to gardening. That's just fine, and it's how most of us start out. But as we plant more extensive gardens, we realize that experience is valuable, and recording all the details makes for a more rewarding and successful gardening experience.

Using a gardening journal helps you keep up with all those important details and plan things better. By keeping a record, you improve your gardens and avoid repeating those inevitable mistakes. Jotting things down all in one place (instead of on hundreds of slips of paper) helps you take stock of each year's gardening progress.

To make it easy for you, we've arranged this Journal into sections: Planning, Weekly Journals, Planting Records and Resources. We've provided the outline and a number of templates. Each section has ideas on how to get the most out of it, plus plant profiles, tips, Club notes and reminders. We've also included a valuable reference section.

You'll find that keeping a garden journal is a habit that pays off. As you fill in these pages, you will become the author of a very personalized and valuable story—one that features you and your garden on every page.

PLANNING
Your Garden on Paper

It's easy to see our gardens in our minds. We almost always see the best things: the patch of ripe tomatoes, warm to the touch; a flawless perennial border that ripples with color; a green, cooling hosta bed in a shady corner. But when we try to map out our plans, reality slips in. There's the neighbor's fence, shading an entire side of the yard for hours each day and keeping rain off your borders. That white garage wall creates a hot mini-climate in the afternoon. And there's the big oak that gives soft, dappled shade until May, when it darkens everything below.

Making a record of your layout gives you the framework on which you build your garden and living areas. Add to that the conditions you grow in—rainfall and frost patterns, soil conditions, temperature range—and you find yourself drawing a picture of your garden. With the maps and grids we've provided here, you can change that picture as you see fit, to bring out the best.

Sample Seasonal Gardening Calendar

	JAN.	FEB.	MAR.	APR.	MAY	JUN.	JUL.	AUG.	SEP.	OCT.	NOV.	DEC.
CONIFERS AND EVERGREENS	■	■	■	■	■	■	■	■	■	■	■	■
EARLY FLOWERING SHRUBS			■	■	■							
SPRING BULBS			■	■								
WILDFLOWERS				■	■	■						
PERENNIALS				■	■	■	■	■	■ (TO FROST)	■		
HERBS				■	■	■	■	■				
TENDER VEGETABLES					■	■	■	■	■			
IRIS				■	■	■						
AZALEAS				■	■							
LILACS				■	■							
HOSTAS				■	■	■	■	■				
PEONIES				■	■							
RASPBERRIES & BRAMBLES					■	■	■					
SECOND SOWINGS FOR FALL CROPS					■	■	■	■				
ANNUALS					■	■	■	■	■			
LILIES					■	■	■					
CLEMATIS						■	■	■	■			
DAYLILIES						■	■	■				
PRAIRIE WILDFLOWERS						■	■	■	■			
CHRYSANTHEMUMS							■	■	■	■		
DAHLIAS							■	■	■			
FRUIT HARVEST							■	■	■	■		
ORNAMENTAL FRUITS	■									■	■	■
FALL COLOR										■	■	
BIRDS MIGRATE			■	■							■	■
SEED CATALOGS ARRIVE	■											
FALL CATALOGS ARRIVE							■					

Start with the Seasons

Every garden has overlapping seasons. Spring bulbs bloom and fade, then daylilies and perennials come along. Birds, bees, and butterflies come and go. This seasonal calendar gives you a way to track the length and timing of these happenings. Use the form on page 7 to track the seasons in your garden.

My Garden's Seasonal Calendar

Using page 6 as an example, fill in the date ranges of bloom times and other gardening events on this page.
This will give you an at-a-glance picture of your garden's seasonal rhythms.

JAN.	FEB.	MAR.	APR.	MAY	JUN.	JUL.	AUG.	SEP.	OCT.	NOV.	DEC.

Drawing a Garden Plan

A) *A plan takes you from paper to planting.*

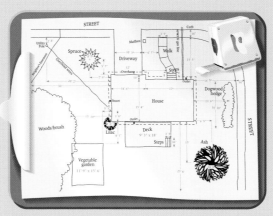

B) *A base map gives you parameters and a detailed overview of your property.*

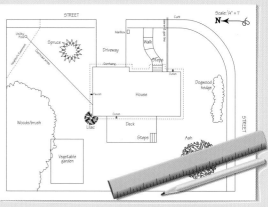

C) *On graph paper, transfer the outlines of physical features to get a scaled-down picture of your layout. Make several copies.*

D) *Walk around and see if your plan makes sense visually. Make any final adjustments.*

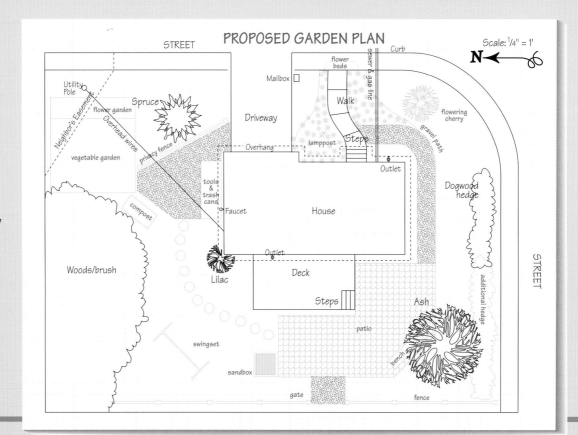

PROPOSED GARDEN PLAN

Scale: ¼" = 1'

STREET

Curb

N

Utility Pole

Neighbor's Easement

Overhead wires

flower garden

Spruce

privacy fence

vegetable garden

tools & trash cans

compost

Faucet

Woods/brush

Lilac

Mailbox

flower beds

Walk

Driveway

lamppost

Steps

Overhang

Outlet

House

sewer & gas line

flowering cherry

gravel path

Dogwood hedge

Outlet

Deck

Steps

Ash

patio

additional hedge

swingset

sandbox

bench

gate

fence

STREET

A Smaller Family Garden

2400 SQ. FT. GARDEN. 12' by 20' plots are divided by access planks into 4' by 12' beds, which are rotated among the main crop groups.

FUNCTIONAL PERIMETER BEDS. Even the edges can be planted in vegetables, fruits, herbs and flowers.

ARBOR. A small picnic table in the arbor allows meals to be served in this beautiful setting.

CORNER FRUIT BUSHES. Depending on your region, you might plant blueberries, dwarf peaches or dwarf cherries.

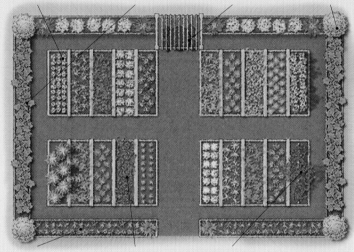

LOWER FRONT PLANTINGS. Herbs and strawberries produce well without blocking an enjoyable view in or out of the garden.

TRELLISED CROPS. Tomatoes, cucumbers, beans, peas and melons make the most of what little ground they use.

HEDGING PLANTS. Raspberries and asparagus are worth fairly large plantings, to avoid buying this costly produce in the store.

LARGE YIELDS FROM A SMALL AREA. Salad and root crops yield a lot on a square-foot basis, and well-planned successions improve yields too.

A Kitchen Garden

BERRIES. Raspberries, blueberries or strawberries could go in the last two beds, out of the way of spring preparation.

PRODUCTION-ORIENTED. Even a practical space will be quite attractive if well maintained.

COMPOST BIN. A large, practical garden will produce plenty of material to compost.

PLANTING BEDS. The beds are formed each spring prior to planting, and the crops rotated among them.

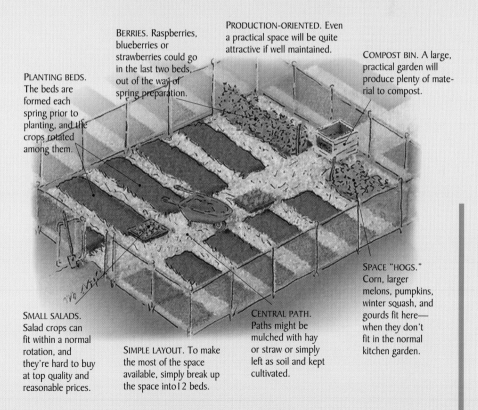

SMALL SALADS. Salad crops can fit within a normal rotation, and they're hard to buy at top quality and reasonable prices.

SIMPLE LAYOUT. To make the most of the space available, simply break up the space into 12 beds.

CENTRAL PATH. Paths might be mulched with hay or straw or simply left as soil and kept cultivated.

SPACE "HOGS." Corn, larger melons, pumpkins, winter squash, and gourds fit here—when they don't fit in the normal kitchen garden.

Sample Garden Designs

A Garden for Everyone

PERMANENT BEDS. Working within defined activity areas makes the garden more beautiful, and the rotation and planting possibilities increase.

HARD SURFACE PATH. For low maintenance and a more passive form of involvement, a brick or stone path permits easy, mud-free access to the beds.

ORNAMENT. In the center, where the paths cross, we might find a sundial, birdbath or a favorite garden ornament.

ENCLOSURE. A partly porous fence, such as a picket fence or lattice, allows just enough air through to still air currents while blocking the major force of the wind.

SALAD VEGETABLES. In this size garden it may make sense to concentrate on growing primarily those things you want to cook with but simply can't buy locally.

HERBS. A large variety of flowers and herbs could be interplanted or could edge the main beds.

EDIBLE FLOWERS. In a kitchen garden, plants like gem marigolds and nasturtiums serve the dual purpose of beauty and food production.

FRAGRANT AND CUTTING FLOWERS. When space is limited, concentrate on special favorites of the gardeners.

FRUIT BUSHES. In the four corners might be blueberries or even trellis-trained currants or gooseberries for visual impact and to make special preserves for Christmas gifts.

A Deck/Container Garden

LARGE CONTAINERS. Half wine barrels or specially made boxes are heavy. They should be on casters for easy moving over the seasons.

PLANTING BOXES. The four planting boxes are treated just like garden plots. They are rotated among crops that can grow in very tight quarters and grow in quick succession, like small salad greens.

AN OUTDOOR ROOM. The key to this design is to make the path from the stairs to the seat serpentine; use plants to do so.

TRELLISED CROPS. One planter box should support a trellis, which permits cultivation of crops like tomatoes, peas, beans and even smaller melons.

SMALL CONTAINERS. With intensive planting, you can get a surprising number of plants in these containers. They are suitable for fresh herbs, edible flowers and some of the smaller fragrant flowers.

PRIVACY DIVIDER. One planter box forms the divider between the inner and outer parts of the deck.

OUTDOOR DINING. The bench and table can be used for outdoor dining, with fresh ingredients close to the kitchen door.

FREQUENT WATERING. If you will not be home during business trips, weekends or vacations, install a drip irrigation system, because containers go dry quickly.

Recording the basics of your garden site gives you a good benchmark. Here's a checklist to work with—or modify if you wish—to make your garden reach its full beauty and potential.

WHAT'S GROWING HERE NOW?

Record here your house, trees, hedges, vines, outbuildings and other in-place features. Include such unattractive things as wild vines, seasonal weeds and bare patches that need attention. Add these elements to the planning grids on pages 12-16—or picture your garden without them in future designs.

WHAT'S MY EXPOSURE?

Mark your garden plot's orientation to the sun and wind. Note areas where plants get windburn in winter and where you might want to plant a protective hedge; or where plants benefit from cooling breezes in the summer.

WHAT'S MY SOIL LIKE?

Do you have heavy clay or dry sandy spots? An area of backfill next to the house? Pockets that don't dry out? Is your soil thin on nutrients? List these conditions so you'll know where to build up your soil.

MY SOIL'S PH:

OTHER NOTES:

WHAT'S MY MOISTURE AND DRAINAGE?

Does water collect where your yard slopes? Do large trees soak up the rain, making an arid region on the ground below? Or do fences, walls, and eaves block rainfall on your beds? Note these conditions here so you know which areas need extra water, and which don't.

GET YOUR SOIL TESTED!

Every gardener should know the pH and nutrient level of his or her soil. Call your county extension agency to arrange a soil test—it's simple and inexpensive, but it pays dividends a hundred times over. You can also use a testing kit or a commercial soil testing company. Any way you do it, get as complete a profile of your garden soil as you can. Then amend as necessary (remember, there's no such thing as too much organic matter in the soil).

Garden Plans

Scale=   to

Scale=   to

Garden Plans

Scale= to

Scale=   to

Garden Plans

Scale=   to

Keeping Your
GARDEN
JOURNAL

This section contains week-by-week information sheets for you to fill in as the year progresses. (A ballpoint pen works the best.) This section also includes profiles on great garden performers, how-to tips and Club notes. At the bottom of each page are seasonal reminders based on broad hardiness zones as listed below. These are just suggestions, so feel free to add your own reminders to customize your journal entries.

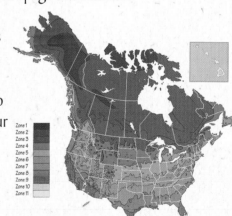

Zone 1
Zone 2
Zone 3
Zone 4
Zone 5
Zone 6
Zone 7
Zone 8
Zone 9
Zone 10
Zone 11

HOT CLIMATE
(ZONES 9-11)

WARM CLIMATE
(ZONES 7-8)

MILD CLIMATE
(ZONES 5-6)

COOL CLIMATE
(ZONES 3-4)

Sterilized, recycled seed-starting equipment will work fine when you start this year's garden. Keep detailed records of your efforts on pp. 52-64.

DON'T BE SOW IMPATIENT...
Unless you need a *really* early start on the season, these veggies and herbs grow better when you plant them directly in the ground: beans, carrots, corn, lettuce, peas, radishes, spinach, sunflowers, dill and fennel.

HOW'S THE WEATHER AND PRECIPITATION?

HOW'S THE SOIL?

WHAT'S BLOOMING?

WHAT AM I PLANTING? (Enter detailed notes in Planting Records section.)

INDOORS

OUTDOORS

WHAT AM I HARVESTING?

WHAT'S GOING ON WITH THE:

FLOWER GARDENS

VEGETABLES & FRUITS

HERBS

TREES & SHRUBS

LAWN

WILDLIFE IN THE GARDEN

OTHER NOTES:

GARDENING CLIMATE REMINDERS:

HOT: Get tools and equipment ready for intense spring work. Clean and repair bird houses. Water early in the morning to prevent fungus and other diseases.

WARM: Order seeds and summer-flowering bulbs. Indoors, start seeds of vegetables, annuals and herbs. Mulch perennials and shrubs after a hard frost.

HOW'S THE WEATHER AND PRECIPITATION?

HOW'S THE SOIL?

WHAT'S BLOOMING?

WHAT AM I PLANTING? (Enter detailed notes in Planting Records section.)
    INDOORS

    OUTDOORS

WHAT AM I HARVESTING?

WHAT'S GOING ON WITH THE:
    FLOWER GARDENS

    VEGETABLES & FRUITS

    HERBS

    TREES & SHRUBS

    LAWN

    WILDLIFE IN THE GARDEN

OTHER NOTES:

INDOOR SEED-STARTING IS EASY...

If you have a few essentials. It doesn't take much—just a good seed-starter mix, various containers and the right environment. Start your seeds in a sterile, peat-based soil-less mix (found at garden centers and mail order suppliers). Use plastic flats or pots, styrofoam containers, peat pots or peat pellets (Jiffy-7s or Jiffy-9s) to hold your mix. Set up in a warm, airy place—most seeds like it around 75°F—or use a heating cable or pad under the flats. Keep seeds dark until they sprout, then give them a steady supply of light so they'll grow strong and stocky. Once the first sets of true leaves grow out, you can transplant.

IT'S YOUR CLUB:

Check out the dozens of new plant listings in the special New Varieties issue—the January-February *Gardening How-To*.

MILD: Study the "bones" of the garden in the winter. Plan your bedding/seating/entertaining areas for the coming season. Order seeds and summer-flowering bulbs.

COOL: Order seeds and summer-flowering bulbs. Break up ice or use immersion heaters to provide water for birds all winter long.

JANUARY

TRY HEIRLOOMS

If you want to grow tried-and-true varieties or if you plan to save your own seed from your plants, heirlooms are a good bet. An heirloom is a plant variety that has stabilized its genetic makeup over the years, so that its qualities—taste, color, and growth habit, for example—reproduce "true" from seed each time it's planted. To be a true heirloom, the variety must have been introduced over 50 years ago. Heirlooms are also called "open-pollinated" varieties, which means that you can count on them to bloom or set a crop of fruits naturally. They depend on insects, birds, animals or the wind to pollinate them.

IT'S YOUR CLUB:

Looking for hard-to-find seeds? Got a seed surplus? Just want to find gardening pen pals or members in your area? That's what Swap Meet is all about. Check out Member to Member, Seed Swap and Seed Search on your Club web site, www.gardeningclub.com.

HOW'S THE WEATHER AND PRECIPITATION?

HOW'S THE SOIL?

WHAT'S BLOOMING?

WHAT AM I PLANTING? (Enter detailed notes in Planting Records section.)
INDOORS

OUTDOORS

WHAT AM I HARVESTING?

WHAT'S GOING ON WITH THE:
FLOWER GARDENS

VEGETABLES & FRUITS

HERBS

TREES & SHRUBS

LAWN

WILDLIFE IN THE GARDEN

OTHER NOTES:

GARDENING CLIMATE REMINDERS:

HOT: Start seeds of hardy vegetables, annuals, and herbs outdoors. Aerate and feed the lawn. Harvest fruits and vegetables daily to foil critters and to promote new production.

WARM: Clean and sharpen your tools and equipment for spring. Protect plants against late-season frost. Clean and repair your bird houses.

HOW'S THE WEATHER AND PRECIPITATION?

HOW'S THE SOIL?

WHAT'S BLOOMING?

WHAT AM I PLANTING? (Enter detailed notes in Planting Records section.)
>INDOORS

>OUTDOORS

WHAT AM I HARVESTING?

WHAT'S GOING ON WITH THE:
>FLOWER GARDENS

>VEGETABLES & FRUITS

>HERBS

>TREES & SHRUBS

>LAWN

>WILDLIFE IN THE GARDEN

OTHER NOTES:

Heirloom beans are easy to grow and have beautiful patterns. Kids and veteran gardeners alike love to grow them for color and flavor.

GRANDMA KNEW 'EM
'Scarlet Runner' and 'Jacob's Cattle' beans, 'Country Gentleman' sweet corn, 'Little Marvel' peas, and 'Brandywine' and 'Mortgage Lifter' tomatoes, are all good examples of the hundreds of heirloom vegetables that have met the test of time (and taste).

MILD: Indoors, start seeds of vegetables, annuals and herbs. Use sterile mixes to prevent damping off of young seedlings.

COOL: Get seed-starting equipment ready, including sterile mixes, trays, pots and lights. Be patient—spring will come! Repot any house plants that need more growing room.

LEAF 'EM ALONE

When bulbs bloom and their foliage begins to fade, it's tempting to cut the leaves or bind them together. But hold off—the leaves need to keep producing food which the bulbs store to support next year's bloom. Don't cut bulb foliage until it turns yellow and drops over. If it's unsightly, plant perennials and annuals around your bulbs to mask the faded foliage. Daylilies are great for this.

Narcissus 'Quail' is just one of hundreds of daffodil varieties you can grow. Mix them with purple muscari for a vibrant color display.

HOW'S THE WEATHER AND PRECIPITATION?

HOW'S THE SOIL?

WHAT'S BLOOMING?

WHAT AM I PLANTING? (Enter detailed notes in Planting Records section.)
    INDOORS

    OUTDOORS

WHAT AM I HARVESTING?

WHAT'S GOING ON WITH THE:
    FLOWER GARDENS

    VEGETABLES & FRUITS

    HERBS

    TREES & SHRUBS

    LAWN

    WILDLIFE IN THE GARDEN

OTHER NOTES:

GARDENING CLIMATE REMINDERS:

HOT: Make compost with organic matter, garden waste and kitchen scraps. Plant fruiting berries, shrubs and trees for wildlife habitat. Side-dress vegetables, perennials, vines, shrubs and trees with compost or balanced, slow-release fertilizer.

WARM: Start seeds of hardy vegetables, annuals and herbs outdoors. Protect against late frosts with overturned pots, blankets, tarps, layers of plastic or other frost-protecting devices.

HOW'S THE WEATHER AND PRECIPITATION?

HOW'S THE SOIL?

WHAT'S BLOOMING?

WHAT AM I PLANTING? (Enter detailed notes in Planting Records section.)
    INDOORS

    OUTDOORS

WHAT AM I HARVESTING?

WHAT'S GOING ON WITH THE:
    FLOWER GARDENS

    VEGETABLES & FRUITS

    HERBS

    TREES & SHRUBS

    LAWN

    WILDLIFE IN THE GARDEN

OTHER NOTES:

MILD: Get your tools and equipment ready for spring. Transplant young seedlings to larger containers after the first set of true leaves grows out.

COOL: Start seeds indoors of vegetables, annuals and herbs. Clean bird feeders at least twice monthly and stock up on bird seed.

ADD SPRING TO YOUR STEP

Nothing says Spring like early bulbs—colorful, cheery crocuses, daffodils, tulips and hyacinths. And they're easy to grow: Usually, once they're established, you never touch them again except to ease overcrowding or propagate more plants. Here are some less-common bulbs that will add variety to your spring garden: winter aconites (*Eranthis* spp.), checkered lily (*Fritillaria meleagris*), glory-of-the-snow (*Chionodoxa* spp.), grape hyacinths (*Muscari* spp.), squills (*Scilla* spp.), snowdrops (*Galanthus* spp.) and dwarf iris (*Iris histroides, I. reticulata*).

In general, spring bulbs are hardy in Zones 3-8; in warmer climates you must "winterize" them in a refrigerator to give them a dormant period.

IT'S YOUR CLUB:

Plan visits to botanical gardens to see how the pros use new ideas on plants, designs and techniques. Get a copy of NHGC's *Directory of Public Gardens* by writing NHGC Member Services Dept., P.O. Box 3401, Minnetonka, MN 55343 or calling (800) 324-8454.

M A R C H

IT'S FOR THE BIRDS

To attract songbirds to your yard, you need three things: water, food and shelter. Set out a birdbath or create a backyard pool for a constant water supply. Place the water supply at least 10 feet away from close cover where cats and other predators may hide. Clean birdbaths every week; in colder areas use an immersion heater to keep water ice-free. For food and shelter, plant fruiting trees and shrubs or evergreens. Use bird feeders to supplement birds' natural diets. Feeders with black-oil sunflower seeds attract a wide range of songbirds including chickadees, nuthatches, woodpeckers, cardinals, jays, grosbeaks, finches, juncos and titmice.

HOW'S THE WEATHER AND PRECIPITATION?

HOW'S THE SOIL?

WHAT'S BLOOMING?

WHAT AM I PLANTING? (Enter detailed notes in Planting Records section.)

    INDOORS

    OUTDOORS

WHAT AM I HARVESTING?

WHAT'S GOING ON WITH THE:

    FLOWER GARDENS

    VEGETABLES & FRUITS

    HERBS

    TREES & SHRUBS

    LAWN

    WILDLIFE IN THE GARDEN

OTHER NOTES:

GARDENING CLIMATE REMINDERS:

HOT: Add 4-6 inches of mulch to keep soil temperatures moderate and conserve moisture. Plant shrub and mini-roses (try minis in containers for portable color). Deadhead annuals and perennials to promote reblooming.

WARM: Aerate and feed the lawn. Harden off tender house, bedding and seedling plants. Plant annual vines for quick-growing shade and privacy or to fill in gaps in the garden.

HOW'S THE WEATHER AND PRECIPITATION?

HOW'S THE SOIL?

WHAT'S BLOOMING?

WHAT AM I PLANTING? (Enter detailed notes in Planting Records section.)
   INDOORS

   OUTDOORS

WHAT AM I HARVESTING?

WHAT'S GOING ON WITH THE:
   FLOWER GARDENS

   VEGETABLES & FRUITS

   HERBS

   TREES & SHRUBS

   LAWN

   WILDLIFE IN THE GARDEN

OTHER NOTES:

CHIRP CITY
To create habitat (food, shelter and nesting sites) for birds, grow these plants: crabapples, serviceberries (*Amelanchier* spp.), hollies, mahonias, pines, spruces, firs, viburnums, hawthorns, bayberries and bearberries.

Serviceberries are well named: They serve up fragrant spring flowers, colorful fruit for birds (and gardeners), and brilliant fall leaf color.

MILD: Start seeds of hardy vegetables, annuals and herbs outdoors. Clean and repair bird houses.

COOL: Transplant young indoor seedlings to larger containers. Take in your local home and garden shows to get a mental jump on spring.

MARCH

Is it an orchid? A lily? No, it's a humble—yet stunning—catalpa tree with its exotic-looking blooms. They smell sweet, too.

HOW'S THE WEATHER AND PRECIPITATION?

HOW'S THE SOIL?

WHAT'S BLOOMING?

WHAT AM I PLANTING? (Enter detailed notes in Planting Records section.)
   INDOORS

   OUTDOORS

WHAT AM I HARVESTING?

WHAT'S GOING ON WITH THE:
   FLOWER GARDENS

   VEGETABLES & FRUITS

   HERBS

   TREES & SHRUBS

   LAWN

   WILDLIFE IN THE GARDEN

OTHER NOTES:

MAKE THAT A $200 HOLE

They used to say "Dig a ten-dollar hole for a one-dollar tree." Even with inflation, the rule hasn't changed. When planting a tree, dig a hole twice as wide as the root ball. Roughen the edges with a fork. Place the ball on a plateau of soil and spread the roots out into the hole. Backfill with soil mixed with lots of organic matter. Make a rim of soil around the hole and water well.

GARDENING CLIMATE REMINDERS:

HOT: To avoid burning your lawn, reduce mowing frequency and raise the height of your lawn mower when hot weather arrives. Look for bargain and markdown trees, perennials and annuals in nurseries and garden centers. Pinch back herbs and annuals to promote branching and more production.

WARM: Set up feeder stations for the birds. Plant fruiting berries, shrubs and trees for wildlife. Plant heat-hardy shrub- and mini-roses (in containers). Prune flowering shrubs—lilacs, forsythia and witch hazel, for example—right after they bloom.

HOW'S THE WEATHER AND PRECIPITATION?

HOW'S THE SOIL?

WHAT'S BLOOMING?

WHAT AM I PLANTING? (Enter detailed notes in Planting Records section.)
    INDOORS

    OUTDOORS

WHAT AM I HARVESTING?

WHAT'S GOING ON WITH THE:
    FLOWER GARDENS

    VEGETABLES & FRUITS

    HERBS

    TREES & SHRUBS

    LAWN

    WILDLIFE IN THE GARDEN

OTHER NOTES:

HUG *THESE* TREES
Arbor Day is near and planting trees is on your mind. Oaks, maples, ashes, pines, firs and spruces fit into just about any landscape. But how about planting something different? Here are some wonderful trees that will become eye-catchers in most environments, while providing excellent shade, fall color or wildlife habitat: ginkgo (*Ginkgo biloba*), serviceberries (*Amelanchier* spp.), catalpas (*Catalpa* spp.), birches (*Betula* spp.), hollies (*Ilex* spp.), beeches (*Fagus* spp.), hornbeams (*Carpinus* spp.), hawthorns (*Crataegus* spp.), sweet gums (*Liquidambar* spp.), paperbark maple (*Acer griseum*) and yellowwood (*Cladrastis lutea*).

MILD: Aerate and feed the lawn. Harden off tender house, bedding and seedling plants with gradual exposure to the outdoors.

COOL: Are your tools and equipment clean and sharpened for spring? Clean and repair bird houses for the arrival of the spring birds, such as bluebirds. Put the houses out now, to be sure they're ready as birds arrive.

LUSCIOUS LILIES

Few flowers are as elegant as lilies, whether they're colorful Asiatic hybrids, ultra-fragrant regals (*Lilium regale*), trumpet-shaped Madonnas or glorious, scented Oriental hybrids. True lilies grow from scaled bulbs (unlike daylilies, which are rhizomes) that will multiply. Give them "cool feet, warm heads" by planting annuals or ground-covers at their base and providing lots of organic mulch. They'll take full sun in most areas, but dappled shade is less likely to fade their colors. Favorite varieties include 'Enchantment', 'Connecticut King', 'Casa Blanca', 'Stargazer' and *L. speciosum* 'Rubrum' and 'Album'. Lilies will grow in all zones (they do well in containers too), but need winter chill in warmest areas.

IT'S YOUR CLUB:

So many new tools, products and plants! If you'd like a chance to try out, report on and keep a new plant or gardening product, request a Product Test Profile form from: National Home Gardening Club, Member Services Dept., P.O. Box 3401, Minnetonka, MN 55343.

HOW'S THE WEATHER AND PRECIPITATION?

HOW'S THE SOIL?

WHAT'S BLOOMING?

WHAT AM I PLANTING? (Enter detailed notes in Planting Records section.)
  INDOORS

  OUTDOORS

WHAT AM I HARVESTING?

WHAT'S GOING ON WITH THE:
  FLOWER GARDENS

  VEGETABLES & FRUITS

  HERBS

  TREES & SHRUBS

  LAWN

  WILDLIFE IN THE GARDEN

OTHER NOTES:

GARDENING CLIMATE REMINDERS:

HOT: Clean bird feeders at least twice monthly, and hummingbird feeders weekly. Check out your local native plants and wildflowers that you can add to your garden. They are truly low-maintenance!

WARM: Make compost with organic matter, garden waste and kitchen scraps. Mulch well to keep soil temperatures moderate and conserve moisture. Deadhead annuals and perennials to promote reblooming.

HOW'S THE WEATHER AND PRECIPITATION?

HOW'S THE SOIL?

WHAT'S BLOOMING?

WHAT AM I PLANTING? (Enter detailed notes in Planting Records section.)
   INDOORS

   OUTDOORS

WHAT AM I HARVESTING?

WHAT'S GOING ON WITH THE:
   FLOWER GARDENS

   VEGETABLES & FRUITS

   HERBS

   TREES & SHRUBS

   LAWN

   WILDLIFE IN THE GARDEN

OTHER NOTES:

GO LIGHT FOR LILIES
Lilies don't need extra-fertile soil. Too much feeding makes for weak stems that need staking. But they do need excellent drainage and consistent moisture, so be sure that your soil is full of organic matter.

Red, pink, orange, silver and striped lilies join with purple delphiniums to create a bold and bright summer display.

MILD: Protect plants against late frost. Prune flowering shrubs right after they bloom: for example lilacs, forsythia and witch hazel.

COOL: Finally! Start seeds of hardy vegetables, annuals and herbs outdoors. If spring comes early, begin to harden off tender house, bedding and seedling plants.

APRIL

Off-white climbing roses like fragrant 'New Dawn' work well with bright clematis varieties. Provide both with sturdy supports and fasten them well.

HOW'S THE WEATHER AND PRECIPITATION?

HOW'S THE SOIL?

WHAT'S BLOOMING?

WHAT AM I PLANTING? (Enter detailed notes in Planting Records section.)

INDOORS

OUTDOORS

WHAT AM I HARVESTING?

WHAT'S GOING ON WITH THE:

FLOWER GARDENS

VEGETABLES & FRUITS

HERBS

TREES & SHRUBS

LAWN

WILDLIFE IN THE GARDEN

OTHER NOTES:

IT'S YOUR CLUB:
Know of a new garden, festival or great garden event coming up? E-mail editors@gardeningclub.com and we'll consider it for the Club web site.

GARDENING CLIMATE REMINDERS:

HOT: Conserve your water with mulching, and water early in the day. Harvest and dry herbs for year-round use.

WARM: Harvest fruits and vegetables daily to foil critters and to promote new production. Clean bird feeders at least twice monthly; hummingbird feeders weekly. Side-dress vegetables, perennials, vines, shrubs trees with compost or balanced, slow-release fertilizer.

HOW'S THE WEATHER AND PRECIPITATION?

HOW'S THE SOIL?

WHAT'S BLOOMING?

WHAT AM I PLANTING? (Enter detailed notes in Planting Records section.)
  INDOORS

  OUTDOORS

WHAT AM I HARVESTING?

WHAT'S GOING ON WITH THE:
  FLOWER GARDENS

  VEGETABLES & FRUITS

  HERBS

  TREES & SHRUBS

  LAWN

  WILDLIFE IN THE GARDEN

OTHER NOTES:

MILD: Plant fruiting berries, shrubs and trees for wildlife. Plant shrub- and mini-roses (in containers for portable color and fragrance). Plant annual vines for quick-growing shade and privacy or to fill in gaps in the garden.

COOL: Protect plants against late frost. Aerate and feed the lawn. Prune flowering shrubs right after they bloom, for example lilacs, forsythia and witch hazel.

MAY

ROSES FOR EVERYONE
Growing roses no longer means fuss and bother. New low-maintenance types—including modern shrub roses, English roses, miniatures, groundcovers and landscape roses—give the home gardener hundreds of choices, especially when you include the offerings of mail order nurseries. Whichever roses you choose, you can minimize problems by buying only certified disease-free stock. Give roses plenty of space—2 to 4 feet between plants—for good air circulation. To prevent splashing disease spores onto foliage, mulch roses well and water deeply at the soil level, not the foliage (soaker hoses and drip systems are great for this). A moderately rich soil with good drainage is best. Feedings in early spring, after first bloom and in early fall should provide plenty of nutrition.

GOOD COMPANY
Try planting clematis with your roses. The clematis will twine through the rose foliage and in most cases will bloom after the first rose flush. You'll get twice as much bloom for the space. Expect people to ask about that strange climbing rose!

QUICK-GROWING VINES

If you want a living, flowering screen to add shade and privacy to your outdoor living areas, plant annual vines. Some good choices, along with their flower colors: black-eyed Susan vine (*Thunbergia alata*)—yellow, orange, or white; cardinal climber (*Ipomoea* x *multifida*)—red; morning glories (*Ipomoea* spp.)—white, blue, red to purple; hyacinth bean (*Dolichos lablab*)—purple; and scarlet runner beans (*Phaseolus coccineus*)—bright red. Hyacinth and scarlet runner beans are edible and lots of fun for kids to grow, too. Provide support with a trellis or a lattice of poles and twine.

HOW'S THE WEATHER AND PRECIPITATION?

HOW'S THE SOIL?

WHAT'S BLOOMING?

WHAT AM I PLANTING? (Enter detailed notes in Planting Records section.)
INDOORS

OUTDOORS

WHAT AM I HARVESTING?

WHAT'S GOING ON WITH THE:
FLOWER GARDENS

VEGETABLES & FRUITS

HERBS

TREES & SHRUBS

LAWN

WILDLIFE IN THE GARDEN

OTHER NOTES:

GARDENING CLIMATE REMINDERS:

HOT: Divide perennials and spring-flowering bulbs (irises, narcissus, alliums, etc.). Replenish mulch where necessary to keep soil temperatures moderate and conserve moisture.

WARM: To avoid burning your lawn, reduce mowing frequency and raise the height of your lawn mower when hot weather arrives. Look for bargain/markdown perennials and annuals in nurseries and garden centers. Check out local native plants and wildflowers that you can add to your garden.

HOW'S THE WEATHER AND PRECIPITATION?

HOW'S THE SOIL?

WHAT'S BLOOMING?

WHAT AM I PLANTING? (Enter detailed notes in Planting Records section.)
   INDOORS

   OUTDOORS

WHAT AM I HARVESTING?

WHAT'S GOING ON WITH THE:
   FLOWER GARDENS

   VEGETABLES & FRUITS

   HERBS

   TREES & SHRUBS

   LAWN

   WILDLIFE IN THE GARDEN

OTHER NOTES:

MILD: Make compost with organic matter, garden waste and kitchen scraps. Mulch to keep soil temperatures moderate and conserve moisture. Let foliage of spring bulbs die back—don't cut it down.

COOL: Plant fruiting berries, shrubs and trees for wildlife. Plant shrub- and mini-roses (in containers). Plant annual vines for quick-growing shade and privacy or to fill in gaps in the garden.

ONE ENCHANTED EVENING
How about having an exotic, perfumed beauty join you on a summer's evening? Plant moonflowers to climb next to your porch and scent the evening breeze. Each 6-inch white moonflower (*Ipomoea alba*) blooms one glorious night before fading, only to be replaced by multitudes of the next night's fragrant flowers. Hint: nick or soak the seeds for quicker germination.

Purple hyacinth bean is a vigorous annual climber that produces edible pods and beans. Pick pods young for cooking.

MAKE 'EM FEEL AT HOME

For prolonged butterfly visits, plant for succession. Keep a steady supply of nectar flowers coming from spring through fall. Plant in large swaths. Butterflies are more attracted to larger masses of color than dabs of different colors. And try to find single-flowered forms— it's easier for butterflies to slip their proboscis into single flowers to draw nectar.

A Great Spangled Fritillary feeding on a favorite nectar plant, Buddleia davidii *(butterfly bush)* 'Dartmoor'.

HOW'S THE WEATHER AND PRECIPITATION?

HOW'S THE SOIL?

WHAT'S BLOOMING?

WHAT AM I PLANTING? (Enter detailed notes in Planting Records section.)
    INDOORS

    OUTDOORS

WHAT AM I HARVESTING?

WHAT'S GOING ON WITH THE:
    FLOWER GARDENS

    VEGETABLES & FRUITS

    HERBS

    TREES & SHRUBS

    LAWN

    WILDLIFE IN THE GARDEN

OTHER NOTES:

GARDENING CLIMATE REMINDERS:

HOT: Water perennials, trees and shrubs deeply—it's better than frequent, shallow waterings. Check mulch levels.

WARM: Divide perennials and spring-flowering bulbs (irises, narcissus, alliums, etc.) Pinch back herbs, annuals and mums to promote branching and more production.

HOW'S THE WEATHER AND PRECIPITATION?

HOW'S THE SOIL?

WHAT'S BLOOMING?

WHAT AM I PLANTING? (Enter detailed notes in Planting Records section.)
    INDOORS

    OUTDOORS

WHAT AM I HARVESTING?

WHAT'S GOING ON WITH THE:
    FLOWER GARDENS

    VEGETABLES & FRUITS

    HERBS

    TREES & SHRUBS

    LAWN

    WILDLIFE IN THE GARDEN

OTHER NOTES:

A WINGED WELCOME MAT
Like birds, butterflies will come to your garden if you follow a few simple rules. First, no pesticides—they'll kill butterflies. Second, provide water with a shallow bath or an inverted lid set in the ground. Butterflies love to sip water as they sit on a dry spot. Third, plant host plants. Butterflies lay eggs on hosts; the hatched larvae (caterpillars) dine on the plants until metamorphosis. Dill, fennel, parsley, milkweeds, violets, passionflowers, heliotrope, willows and pawpaws are some butterfly host plants. Fourth, find a sunny, calm spot to plant nectar plants: lantanas, asters, phlox, purple coneflowers, tuberoses, scabiosa, butterfly bush (*Buddleia davidii*) and zinnias, for example.

MILD: Clean bird feeders at least twice monthly; hummingbird feeders weekly. Look for bargain/markdown perennials and annuals in nurseries and garden centers. Deadhead annuals and perennials to promote reblooming.

COOL: Make compost with organic matter, garden waste and kitchen scraps. Mulch to keep soil temperatures moderate and conserve moisture. Check out local native plants and wildflowers that you can add to your garden. They're real survivors!

TOP TOMATO TIPS

These natives of Peru are America's favorite home garden crop, with good reason. They're easy to grow and offer a quantum leap in flavor over the grown-for-shipping supermarket offerings. Follow a few tips and your tomatoes will thrive: Choose disease-resistant varieties (but rotate the location of your bed each year). Set plants out deeply, in a sunny spot, when the soil is warm—not before. Mulch well to keep soil temperatures moderate. Water deeply at the ground level. Feed when fruit clusters form and every 2-3 weeks thereafter. Keep fruit off the ground with stakes and ties. Pick fruits just before ripe to foil the squirrels. Don't store tomatoes in the fridge. Enjoy!

TELLING ABOUT TASTE

If you're looking for flavorful, high-producing tomatoes, grow these tried-and-true varieties: 'Better Boy', 'Big Beef', 'Early Girl', 'Heatwave', 'Roma' and 'Sun Gold'; plus the heirlooms 'Brandywine', 'Mortgage Lifter', 'Black Krim', 'Black Prince' and 'Amish Paste'. The heirlooms might be fussier and uglier, but oh that flavor!

HOW'S THE WEATHER AND PRECIPITATION?

HOW'S THE SOIL?

WHAT'S BLOOMING?

WHAT AM I PLANTING? (Enter detailed notes in Planting Records section.)
 INDOORS

 OUTDOORS

WHAT AM I HARVESTING?

WHAT'S GOING ON WITH THE:
 FLOWER GARDENS

 VEGETABLES & FRUITS

 HERBS

 TREES & SHRUBS

 LAWN

 WILDLIFE IN THE GARDEN

OTHER NOTES:

HOW'S THE WEATHER AND PRECIPITATION?

HOW'S THE SOIL?

WHAT'S BLOOMING?

WHAT AM I PLANTING? (Enter detailed notes in Planting Records section.)
>   INDOORS

>   OUTDOORS

WHAT AM I HARVESTING?

WHAT'S GOING ON WITH THE:
>   FLOWER GARDENS

>   VEGETABLES & FRUITS

>   HERBS

>   TREES & SHRUBS

>   LAWN

>   WILDLIFE IN THE GARDEN

OTHER NOTES:

Today's gardener can grow tomatoes that are shaped like grapes, plums, pears, cherries, multi-lobed gourds or even ... tomatoes!

MILD: Reduce mowing frequency and raise the cutting height of your lawn mower when hot weather arrives. Pinch back herbs, annuals and mums to promote branching and more production. Side-dress vegetables, perennials, vines, shrubs and trees with compost or balanced, slow-release fertilizer.

COOL: Look for bargain/markdown perennials and annuals in nurseries and garden centers. Side-dress vegetables, perennials, vines, shrubs and trees with compost or balanced, slow-release fertilizer. Deadhead annuals and perennials to promote reblooming.

IT'S YOUR CLUB:
Proud of the way your garden looks? Did you grow a bumper crop of tomatoes or blueberries? Got a great tip? Throwing a garden party to share your success? Show off! Take a photo and send it to Home Grown, *Gardening How-To*, P.O Box 3401, Minnetonka, MN 55343.

JUNE

PICK AT THEIR PEAK

The best time to pick herbs for drying is just before the plants bloom. Choose an early morning, just after the dew has dried but before the sun dries out the oils. By the way, the flavor of dried herbs is about twice as strong as the same amount of fresh ones, so adjust recipes accordingly.

Place screens in airy, shaded places to dry herbs. Here are basil, lavender, thyme, rosemary and broadleaf Italian parsley.

HOW'S THE WEATHER AND PRECIPITATION?

HOW'S THE SOIL?

WHAT'S BLOOMING?

WHAT AM I PLANTING? (Enter detailed notes in Planting Records section.)

    INDOORS

    OUTDOORS

WHAT AM I HARVESTING?

WHAT'S GOING ON WITH THE:

    FLOWER GARDENS

    VEGETABLES & FRUITS

    HERBS

    TREES & SHRUBS

    LAWN

    WILDLIFE IN THE GARDEN

OTHER NOTES:

GARDENING CLIMATE REMINDERS:

HOT: Plant fruiting berries, shrubs and trees for wildlife habitat. (See the lists on pp. 25, 27 and 35.)

WARM: Harvest and dry herbs for year-round use. Give the remaining herbs a feeding to boost regrowth.

HOW'S THE WEATHER AND PRECIPITATION?

HOW'S THE SOIL?

WHAT'S BLOOMING?

WHAT AM I PLANTING? (Enter detailed notes in Planting Records section.)
    INDOORS

    OUTDOORS

WHAT AM I HARVESTING?

WHAT'S GOING ON WITH THE:
    FLOWER GARDENS

    VEGETABLES & FRUITS

    HERBS

    TREES & SHRUBS

    LAWN

    WILDLIFE IN THE GARDEN

OTHER NOTES:

MILD: Divide perennials and spring-flowering bulbs (irises, narcissus, alliums, etc.). Harvest fruits and vegetables daily to foil critters and promote new production. Replenish mulch as needed to keep soil temperatures moderate and conserve moisture.

COOL: Divide perennials and spring-flowering bulbs (irises, alliums, narcissus, etc.). Pinch back herbs, annuals and mums to promote branching and more production. Water early in the morning to prevent fungus and other diseases.

STORE A CROP OF HERBS

Fresh herbs aren't always available, so here's how you can dry them: Rinse and dry your herbs well. Fasten stems of small bunches with twine or rubber bands. Cut air holes (for ventilation) in a paper bag, and place the herbs inside. The bag keeps dust and bugs off. Twist the mouth of the bag around the stems with a twist-tie and hang the bagged herbs in a dry, airy space. When the leaves are dry (in a week or so), gently strip them off and pour them into clean, dry, airtight jars.

You can also dry herbs in a microwave. Place a layer of herbs between two paper towels. Run the microwave on high, 30 seconds at a time, until the herbs are completely dried. (Watch carefully.) Store the same as air-dried herbs.

IT'S YOUR CLUB:
Something got you stumped? Send questions to Expert Advice, *Gardening How-To*, P.O. Box 3401, Minnetonka, MN 55343, or e-mail questions@gardeningclub.com. We will consider them for the Expert Advice column in the magazine.

JULY

HERE COMES THE SUNFLOWER

They can spring up from birdseed, in the compost heap or in the wilds. But "tame" sunflowers are awfully wild these days. Sunflowers (*Helianthus annuus*) grow with stunning effect in just about any garden setting. There are huge-heading types ('Russian Mammoth', 'Confection'); red and orange tones ('Evening Sun', 'Orange King'); thick-heading doubles ('Dragon's Fire'). Then there's 'Supermane', which can grow 10-inch-wide, 3-inch-thick golden heads that resemble a vegetable lion. There are colorful Mexican sunflowers (*Tithonia rotundifolia*) with orange-red flowers, and vigorous perennials that are great for cutting (*H. maximilianii, H. atrorubens*).

SUNNY DISPOSITIONS

Sunflowers are easy to grow, which makes them great fun for kids and beginners, and time-savers for experienced gardeners. They often self-seed, too. They like full sun (a little shade in the hottest climates wouldn't hurt), regular watering and average well-drained soil. Mulch well to conserve moisture and stake the tallest kinds when you plant.

HOW'S THE WEATHER AND PRECIPITATION?

HOW'S THE SOIL?

WHAT'S BLOOMING?

WHAT AM I PLANTING? (Enter detailed notes in Planting Records section.)
    INDOORS

    OUTDOORS

WHAT AM I HARVESTING?

WHAT'S GOING ON WITH THE:
    FLOWER GARDENS

    VEGETABLES & FRUITS

    HERBS

    TREES & SHRUBS

    LAWN

    WILDLIFE IN THE GARDEN

OTHER NOTES:

GARDENING CLIMATE REMINDERS:

HOT: Set up feeder stations for the birds. Use different feeders for different kinds of seed and hang feeders at varying heights to discourage overcrowding (birds need their space, too!).

WARM: Replenish mulch as needed to keep soil temperatures moderate and conserve moisture.

HOW'S THE WEATHER AND PRECIPITATION?

HOW'S THE SOIL?

WHAT'S BLOOMING?

WHAT AM I PLANTING? (Enter detailed notes in Planting Records section.)
    INDOORS

    OUTDOORS

WHAT AM I HARVESTING?

WHAT'S GOING ON WITH THE:
    FLOWER GARDENS

    VEGETABLES & FRUITS

    HERBS

    TREES & SHRUBS

    LAWN

    WILDLIFE IN THE GARDEN

OTHER NOTES:

You can grow sunflowers whose colors cover the red, orange and yellow side of the garden palette. Here is 'Red Sun'.

MILD: Water perennials, trees and shrubs deeply. Harvest and dry herbs for year-round use. (See pages 38-39 for tips.)

COOL: Late in the month, aerate and feed the lawn for next year. Harvest fruits and vegetables daily to foil critters and to promote new production. Harvest and dry herbs for year-round use. Plant garlic and leeks now for harvest in 6-8 months.

IT'S YOUR CLUB:
Want to learn more about the birds, butterflies, and other wildlife in your garden? The Backyard Wildlife column in every issue of *Gardening How-To* **gives you hints, tips, and advice to attract the wildlife you want in your garden— and get rid of the critters you don't.**

Pictured here is goldenrod 'Fireworks' with salvia 'Indigo Spires' and aster 'Alma Potschke'. For prolonged fall color display, plant goldenrod with mums, sedums, sneezeweed (Helenium spp.), false starwort (Boltonia asteroides) and asters.

I'M INNOCENT!

Goldenrod doesn't cause hay fever. The real culprit is ragweed (*Ambrosia artemisiifolia*), which spews wind-borne allergenic pollen just when goldenrod sets out its clingy pollen for insects to carry. Ragweed pollen contains 23 known allergens.

HOW'S THE WEATHER AND PRECIPITATION?

HOW'S THE SOIL?

WHAT'S BLOOMING?

WHAT AM I PLANTING? (Enter detailed notes in Planting Records section.)
   INDOORS

   OUTDOORS

WHAT AM I HARVESTING?

WHAT'S GOING ON WITH THE:
   FLOWER GARDENS

   VEGETABLES & FRUITS

   HERBS

   TREES & SHRUBS

   LAWN

   WILDLIFE IN THE GARDEN

OTHER NOTES:

GARDENING CLIMATE REMINDERS:

HOT: Start seeds of hardy vegetables, annuals and herbs outdoors. Test your soil to see if it needs amendments or pH adjustment.

WARM: Clean bird feeders at least twice monthly; hummingbird feeders weekly. Keep bird baths clean and full of water. Plant garlic and leeks now for harvest in 6-8 months.

HOW'S THE WEATHER AND PRECIPITATION?

HOW'S THE SOIL?

WHAT'S BLOOMING?

WHAT AM I PLANTING? (Enter detailed notes in Planting Records section.)
    INDOORS

    OUTDOORS

WHAT AM I HARVESTING?

WHAT'S GOING ON WITH THE:
    FLOWER GARDENS

    VEGETABLES & FRUITS

    HERBS

    TREES & SHRUBS

    LAWN

    WILDLIFE IN THE GARDEN

OTHER NOTES:

MILD: Aerate and feed the lawn for next spring's growth. Set up feeder stations for the birds. Plant garlic and leeks now for harvest in 6-8 months.

COOL: Protect plants against early frost. Water perennials, trees and shrubs deeply. Later in the month, spray trees and perennials with antidessicant spray to prevent sunscald or winter burn. Clean up container plants before you bring them indoors. Lift and store tender bulbs (cannas, calla lilies, etc.).

AN AUTUMN ROMANCER

Goldenrod (*Solidago* spp.) is a native perennial that grows almost anywhere in the U.S. It makes a wonderful border or meadow plant that grows easily; feeds birds, butterflies, and hummingbirds; and makes long-lasting cut flowers.

Goldenrod likes lean soil and full sun to light shade. It can be propagated by division or stem cuttings, but it often self-sows. In moist, fertile soils it may become invasive.

More than 100 species of *Solidago* exist. Three terrific garden choices are 'Fireworks', 'Crown of Rays' ('Strahlenkrone') and 'Golden Fleece', a spreading, 18-inch tall version. All three are hardy in Zones 4-9.

IT'S YOUR CLUB:

Looking for unbiased test results on the latest gardening tools, products and plants? Check the Member Tested department in each issue of *Gardening How-To*. You'll find the ratings and comments of your fellow Club members who tried out the products in their gardens, plus a product description and ordering information.

SEPTEMBER

**PUCKER UP
FOR THE HOLIDAYS**

Herbal vinegars are terrific flavor boosters in the holiday kitchen and make nice gifts too. Start with a gallon of good wine vinegar or apple-cider vinegar. Use one part of dried herbs to four parts vinegar—that's 4 cups of dried herbs to a gallon of vinegar. (If using fresh herbs, use twice as much.) Pour the vinegar into a pot or pitcher. Then stuff the herbs into the original vinegar bottle and pour the vinegar back through a funnel. Cap tightly and store in a cool, dark place for 1-4 weeks. When it tastes strong enough, strain and pour the vinegar into clean, dry, decorative bottles. Add sprigs of herbs and cap or cork well.

FORCE THE ISSUE

October is a good time to start bulbs for indoor forcing during the holidays and in winter. Plant a succession of bulbs every two weeks or so.

HOW'S THE WEATHER AND PRECIPITATION?

HOW'S THE SOIL?

WHAT'S BLOOMING?

WHAT AM I PLANTING? (Enter detailed notes in Planting Records section.)
  INDOORS

  OUTDOORS

WHAT AM I HARVESTING?

WHAT'S GOING ON WITH THE:
  FLOWER GARDENS

  VEGETABLES & FRUITS

  HERBS

  TREES & SHRUBS

  LAWN

  WILDLIFE IN THE GARDEN

OTHER NOTES:

GARDENING CLIMATE REMINDERS:

HOT: Harvest fruits and vegetables daily to foil critters and to promote new production. Clean bird feeders at least twice monthly; hummingbird feeders weekly. Side-dress vegetables, perennials, vines, shrubs and trees with compost or balanced, slow-release fertilizer.

WARM: Aerate and feed the lawn for next spring's growth. Test your soil to see if it's depleted. Here's how: Send a soil sample to your county extension office or use a home testing kit.

HOW'S THE WEATHER AND PRECIPITATION?

HOW'S THE SOIL?

WHAT'S BLOOMING?

WHAT AM I PLANTING? (Enter detailed notes in Planting Records section.)
  INDOORS

  OUTDOORS

WHAT AM I HARVESTING?

WHAT'S GOING ON WITH THE:
  FLOWER GARDENS

  VEGETABLES & FRUITS

  HERBS

  TREES & SHRUBS

  LAWN

  WILDLIFE IN THE GARDEN

OTHER NOTES:

MILD: Water perennials, trees and shrubs deeply. Spray with antidessicant spray to prevent sunscald or winter burn. Clean up container plants before you bring them indoors. Check them for insects and damage. Test your soil to see if it needs fall amendments or adjustments. Lift and store tender bulbs (cannas, calla lilies, etc.).

COOL: Repair and winterize equipment. Clean up the garden at the end of season. Set up feeder stations for the birds. Dig up vegetable, annual, herb and perennial beds so they will be ready for planting in the spring.

TART AND TASTY

Some of the best herbs for flavoring vinegars are French tarragon, purple basils (which leave a rose-colored liquid), lavender, rosemary, thyme and lemon grass. You can combine herbs as you would to make kitchen seasonings, for example an Italian mix of basil, oregano, garlic (peeled) and pepper. For an exotic touch, try vinegar flavored with edible 'Lemon Gem' marigolds.

Add a sprig or two of herbs to flavor your vinegars. Keep your bottles out of bright light, or the colors will fade.

IT'S YOUR CLUB:

Every issue of *GHT* includes the Garden Giveaway sweepstakes. That's where you can win great gardening products by going to the Club web site, www.gardeningclub.com

*Areca palm (*Chrysalidocarpus lutescens*) was top-rated for its ability to remove chemicals from indoor air. It's easy to grow too.*

HOW'S THE WEATHER AND PRECIPITATION?

HOW'S THE SOIL?

WHAT'S BLOOMING?

WHAT AM I PLANTING? (Enter detailed notes in Planting Records section.)

INDOORS

OUTDOORS

WHAT AM I HARVESTING?

WHAT'S GOING ON WITH THE:

FLOWER GARDENS

VEGETABLES & FRUITS

HERBS

TREES & SHRUBS

LAWN

WILDLIFE IN THE GARDEN

OTHER NOTES:

CLEANUP CREW

Among the top air-purifiers in NASA studies are bamboo palm (*Chamaedora seifrizii*), rubber plant (*Ficus robusta*), Boston fern (*Nephrolepsis exaltata*), gerbera daisy (*Gerbera jamesonii*), English ivy (*Hedera helix*), dwarf date palm (*Phoenix roebelenii*), peace lily (*Spathiphyllum* spp.) and lady palm (*Rhapsis excelsa*).

GARDENING CLIMATE REMINDERS:

HOT: Aerate and feed the lawn for next year's early growth. Clean up container plants before you bring them indoors. Check them for insects and damage. Harvest and dry herbs for year-round use.

WARM: Water perennials, trees and shrubs deeply. Spray them with antidessicant spray to prevent sunscald or winter burn. Clean up container plants before you bring them indoors. Check for insects and damage. Test your soil for any amendments or adjustments. Lift and store tender bulbs (cannas, calla lilies, gingers, etc.).

HOW'S THE WEATHER AND PRECIPITATION?

HOW'S THE SOIL?

WHAT'S BLOOMING?

WHAT AM I PLANTING? (Enter detailed notes in Planting Records section.)

    INDOORS

    OUTDOORS

WHAT AM I HARVESTING?

WHAT'S GOING ON WITH THE:

    FLOWER GARDENS

    VEGETABLES & FRUITS

    HERBS

    TREES & SHRUBS

    LAWN

    WILDLIFE IN THE GARDEN

OTHER NOTES:

MILD: Repair and winterize equipment and tools. Protect plants against early frost. Clean up the garden at end of season. Dig up vegetable, annual, herb and perennial beds now so they will be ready for planting in the spring.

COOL: Mulch perennials and shrubs after a hard frost. Clean bird feeders at least twice monthly and use fresh seed. Provide water for birds all winter long. Test your soil for any needed amendments.

WHERE NO PLANT HAS GONE BEFORE

Here's a green way to clean your household or office air—grow more house plants. Not just any plants, but the ones that Spock, McCoy and Kirk might grow in the Starship Enterprise. NASA researchers have found that certain indoor plants (see left) purify the air of enclosed environments such as spacecraft, offices and homes. The plants remove such indoor pollutants as formaldehyde and the odors of paints, adhesives, particle board, stains, varnishes, ammonia and alcohol. Researchers in Australia report a link between live indoor plants and people's ability to concentrate and produce on the job. So clear the air—and your head—by growing more indoor plants!

COUNT YOUR BIRDS

Make plans to participate in the Audubon Christmas Bird Count—to find out more, contact the National Audubon Society at www.audubon. org/bird/cbc or 212-979-3000.

NOVEMBER

D E C E M B E R

A PALETTE OF POINSETTIAS

Poinsettias were "discovered" as a native shrub in Mexico by an American diplomat in the 1820s, and have been a big-time holiday symbol since the 1920s. More than 60 million plants are sold in the U.S. each year. Gardeners in very warm climates can grow them as hedges, but the rest of us know them as holiday plants. Advances in breeding have given us many more choices in size and color than the standard red single varieties. Now we can find doubles, pastels, dapples, marbles, pinks, whites—even yellow! Keep your potted holiday poinsettia in a 70° room; keep soil moist but don't let the plant sit in water. In the South, keep plants out of direct sunlight or colors may fade.

IT'S YOUR CLUB:
Your Club web site is located at www.gardeningclub.com. Visit it for Club info, garden tips, members' garden photos, chats with other members, articles, members-only giveaways, discounts, contests, and more.

HOW'S THE WEATHER AND PRECIPITATION?

HOW'S THE SOIL?

WHAT'S BLOOMING?

WHAT AM I PLANTING? (Enter detailed notes in Planting Records section.)
 INDOORS

 OUTDOORS

WHAT AM I HARVESTING?

WHAT'S GOING ON WITH THE:
 FLOWER GARDENS

 VEGETABLES & FRUITS

 HERBS

 TREES & SHRUBS

 LAWN

 WILDLIFE IN THE GARDEN

OTHER NOTES:

HOW'S THE WEATHER AND PRECIPITATION?

HOW'S THE SOIL?

WHAT'S BLOOMING?

WHAT AM I PLANTING? (Enter detailed notes in Planting Records section.)
 INDOORS

 OUTDOORS

WHAT AM I HARVESTING?

WHAT'S GOING ON WITH THE:
 FLOWER GARDENS

 VEGETABLES & FRUITS

 HERBS

 TREES & SHRUBS

 LAWN

 WILDLIFE IN THE GARDEN

OTHER NOTES:

Poinsettia 'Freedom Marble' is a good example of the pastel colors and textures you can find to brighten your winter decor. Or use this beauty as a holiday gift plant.

A BITE OUT OF FOLKLORE
Some people shy away from poinsettias in the belief that the plants are poisonous, but they're not. They do exude a milky, sticky liquid that can irritate the skin or stomach, so keep them away from kids and pets, but eating a leaf isn't deadly. (All the same, don't make a holiday salad out of them!)

MILD: Mulch perennials and shrubs after a hard frost. Clean bird feeders at least twice monthly; use fresh, dry seed. Provide water for birds all winter long.

COOL: Study the framework of your garden in the winter, and plan your future bedding/seating/entertaining areas. Hang out suet feeders for energy-depleted birds and hang an extra feeder for seed.

In Summary...

Did you have a bumper crop of raspberries or a beautiful display of lilies for Mother's Day? Did a rainstorm wash out your newly seeded lawn? Did your 3-year-old perennial bed come into glory this year, or squirrels eat your early tomatoes? Here's a place to tally up the garden year and make notes on how things did. You can record this year's successes—and any disasters that happened—to make next year's garden better.

WHAT WORKED?

FLOWERS

VEGETABLES

HERBS

SHRUBS

TREES

FRUITING PLANTS

WILDLIFE

OTHER

WHAT DIDN'T WORK?

FLOWERS

VEGETABLES

HERBS

SHRUBS

TREES

FRUITING PLANTS

WILDLIFE

OTHER

WHAT WOULD I DO DIFFERENTLY NEXT YEAR?

FLOWERS

VEGETABLES

HERBS

SHRUBS

TREES

FRUITING PLANTS

WILDLIFE

OTHER

GENERAL NOTES ON THE YEAR:

Finally—one place to record all those mental notes about the plants you grow! The next 13 pages will let you make detailed notes on the prize performers in your garden, so you can order more of them or refer them to friends. You can also chronicle the ones that didn't do so well, so you can move them to a different spot or replace them with other plants.

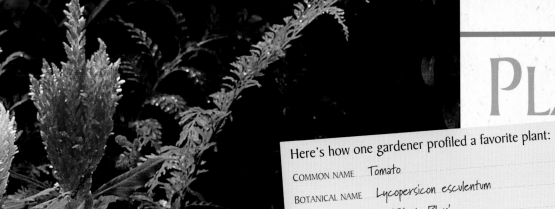

Here's how one gardener profiled a favorite plant:

COMMON NAME   Tomato

BOTANICAL NAME   Lycopersicon esculentum

CULTIVAR OR VARIETY   'Black Plum'

TYPE (annual, perennial, vegetable, flower, etc.)

   Vegetable (Russian variety)

FORM   SEEDS ✔   PLANTS

                            OTHER

BARE-ROOT   CONTAINER

SOURCE   Seed Savers Exchange

DATE PURCHASED OR RECEIVED Ordered: Jan. 10. Rec'd: Jan. 25

COST   1 pkt., $2.50

CONDITION   OK

DATE PLANTED Feb. 2 (in Jiffy-7s) FIRST GERMINATION Feb. 14

TRANSPLANTED 1st Mar. 24 (6-inch pots). Outside: April 22.

LOCATION PLANTED 4 in main veg. patch; 1 in container on

porch. (Gave several plants away to the kids and neighbors)

PROJECTED MATURE SIZE: HEIGHT 6 ft. + SPREAD 2½ ft. (in cage)

BLOOMING/FRUITING PERIOD 1st blooms: May 4.

  1st ripe tomatoes: June 30!

COLOR/FORM/FOLIAGE NOTES Tomatoes were dark orange

to brownish-black

YIELD (FRUITS/VEGETABLES/HERBS) Lots!—at least two dozen per

week, for 16 weeks

HOW DID THIS PLANT PERFORM? Wonderfully. 85% germination rate.

Tolerated a cold snap in late April. Healthy plants (one in

container needed more room). Lots of delicious tomatoes,

great for fresh sauces, fresh eating. Froze many whole;

made some into soup mix for freezer. Neighbors and kids

loved theirs too. Will plant 6 next year!

Planting Records

COMMON NAME

BOTANICAL NAME

CULTIVAR OR VARIETY

TYPE (annual, perennial, vegetable, flower, etc.)

FORM   SEEDS   PLANTS

BARE-ROOT   CONTAINER   OTHER

SOURCE

DATE PURCHASED OR RECEIVED

COST

CONDITION

DATE PLANTED   FIRST GERMINATION

TRANSPLANTED

LOCATION PLANTED

PROJECTED MATURE SIZE: HEIGHT   SPREAD

BLOOMING/FRUITING PERIOD

COLOR/FORM/FOLIAGE NOTES

YIELD (FRUITS/VEGETABLES/HERBS)

HOW DID THIS PLANT PERFORM?

COMMON NAME

BOTANICAL NAME

CULTIVAR OR VARIETY

TYPE (annual, perennial, vegetable, flower, etc.)

FORM   SEEDS   PLANTS

BARE-ROOT   CONTAINER   OTHER

SOURCE

DATE PURCHASED OR RECEIVED

COST

CONDITION

DATE PLANTED   FIRST GERMINATION

TRANSPLANTED

LOCATION PLANTED

PROJECTED MATURE SIZE: HEIGHT   SPREAD

BLOOMING/FRUITING PERIOD

COLOR/FORM/FOLIAGE NOTES

YIELD (FRUITS/VEGETABLES/HERBS)

HOW DID THIS PLANT PERFORM?

COMMON NAME

BOTANICAL NAME

CULTIVAR OR VARIETY

TYPE (annual, perennial, vegetable, flower, etc.)

FORM   SEEDS   PLANTS

BARE-ROOT   CONTAINER   OTHER

SOURCE

DATE PURCHASED OR RECEIVED

COST

CONDITION

DATE PLANTED   FIRST GERMINATION

TRANSPLANTED

LOCATION PLANTED

PROJECTED MATURE SIZE: HEIGHT   SPREAD

BLOOMING/FRUITING PERIOD

COLOR/FORM/FOLIAGE NOTES

YIELD (FRUITS/VEGETABLES/HERBS)

HOW DID THIS PLANT PERFORM?

COMMON NAME

BOTANICAL NAME

CULTIVAR OR VARIETY

TYPE (annual, perennial, vegetable, flower, etc.)

FORM   SEEDS   PLANTS

BARE-ROOT   CONTAINER   OTHER

SOURCE

DATE PURCHASED OR RECEIVED

COST

CONDITION

DATE PLANTED   FIRST GERMINATION

TRANSPLANTED

LOCATION PLANTED

PROJECTED MATURE SIZE: HEIGHT   SPREAD

BLOOMING/FRUITING PERIOD

COLOR/FORM/FOLIAGE NOTES

YIELD (FRUITS/VEGETABLES/HERBS)

HOW DID THIS PLANT PERFORM?

Planting Records

COMMON NAME ....

BOTANICAL NAME ....

CULTIVAR OR VARIETY ....

TYPE (annual, perennial, vegetable, flower, etc.) ....

FORM .... SEEDS .... PLANTS ....

BARE-ROOT .... CONTAINER .... OTHER ....

SOURCE ....

DATE PURCHASED OR RECEIVED ....

COST ....

CONDITION ....

DATE PLANTED .... FIRST GERMINATION ....

TRANSPLANTED ....

LOCATION PLANTED ....

PROJECTED MATURE SIZE: HEIGHT .... SPREAD ....

BLOOMING/FRUITING PERIOD ....

COLOR/FORM/FOLIAGE NOTES ....

YIELD (FRUITS/VEGETABLES/HERBS) ....

HOW DID THIS PLANT PERFORM? ....

COMMON NAME ....

BOTANICAL NAME ....

CULTIVAR OR VARIETY ....

TYPE (annual, perennial, vegetable, flower, etc.) ....

FORM .... SEEDS .... PLANTS ....

BARE-ROOT .... CONTAINER .... OTHER ....

SOURCE ....

DATE PURCHASED OR RECEIVED ....

COST ....

CONDITION ....

DATE PLANTED .... FIRST GERMINATION ....

TRANSPLANTED ....

LOCATION PLANTED ....

PROJECTED MATURE SIZE: HEIGHT .... SPREAD ....

BLOOMING/FRUITING PERIOD ....

COLOR/FORM/FOLIAGE NOTES ....

YIELD (FRUITS/VEGETABLES/HERBS) ....

HOW DID THIS PLANT PERFORM? ....

COMMON NAME

BOTANICAL NAME

CULTIVAR OR VARIETY

TYPE (annual, perennial, vegetable, flower, etc.)

FORM   SEEDS   PLANTS

BARE-ROOT   CONTAINER   OTHER

SOURCE

DATE PURCHASED OR RECEIVED

COST

CONDITION

DATE PLANTED   FIRST GERMINATION

TRANSPLANTED

LOCATION PLANTED

PROJECTED MATURE SIZE: HEIGHT   SPREAD

BLOOMING/FRUITING PERIOD

COLOR/FORM/FOLIAGE NOTES

YIELD (FRUITS/VEGETABLES/HERBS)

HOW DID THIS PLANT PERFORM?

COMMON NAME

BOTANICAL NAME

CULTIVAR OR VARIETY

TYPE (annual, perennial, vegetable, flower, etc.)

FORM   SEEDS   PLANTS

BARE-ROOT   CONTAINER   OTHER

SOURCE

DATE PURCHASED OR RECEIVED

COST

CONDITION

DATE PLANTED   FIRST GERMINATION

TRANSPLANTED

LOCATION PLANTED

PROJECTED MATURE SIZE: HEIGHT   SPREAD

BLOOMING/FRUITING PERIOD

COLOR/FORM/FOLIAGE NOTES

YIELD (FRUITS/VEGETABLES/HERBS)

HOW DID THIS PLANT PERFORM?

Planting Records

COMMON NAME

BOTANICAL NAME

CULTIVAR OR VARIETY

TYPE (annual, perennial, vegetable, flower, etc.)

FORM   SEEDS   PLANTS

BARE-ROOT   CONTAINER   OTHER

SOURCE

DATE PURCHASED OR RECEIVED

COST

CONDITION

DATE PLANTED   FIRST GERMINATION

TRANSPLANTED

LOCATION PLANTED

PROJECTED MATURE SIZE: HEIGHT   SPREAD

BLOOMING/FRUITING PERIOD

COLOR/FORM/FOLIAGE NOTES

YIELD (FRUITS/VEGETABLES/HERBS)

HOW DID THIS PLANT PERFORM?

COMMON NAME

BOTANICAL NAME

CULTIVAR OR VARIETY

TYPE (annual, perennial, vegetable, flower, etc.)

FORM   SEEDS   PLANTS

BARE-ROOT   CONTAINER   OTHER

SOURCE

DATE PURCHASED OR RECEIVED

COST

CONDITION

DATE PLANTED   FIRST GERMINATION

TRANSPLANTED

LOCATION PLANTED

PROJECTED MATURE SIZE: HEIGHT   SPREAD

BLOOMING/FRUITING PERIOD

COLOR/FORM/FOLIAGE NOTES

YIELD (FRUITS/VEGETABLES/HERBS)

HOW DID THIS PLANT PERFORM?

COMMON NAME

BOTANICAL NAME

CULTIVAR OR VARIETY

TYPE (annual, perennial, vegetable, flower, etc.)

FORM   SEEDS   PLANTS

BARE-ROOT   CONTAINER   OTHER

SOURCE

DATE PURCHASED OR RECEIVED

COST

CONDITION

DATE PLANTED   FIRST GERMINATION

TRANSPLANTED

LOCATION PLANTED

PROJECTED MATURE SIZE: HEIGHT   SPREAD

BLOOMING/FRUITING PERIOD

COLOR/FORM/FOLIAGE NOTES

YIELD (FRUITS/VEGETABLES/HERBS)

HOW DID THIS PLANT PERFORM?

COMMON NAME

BOTANICAL NAME

CULTIVAR OR VARIETY

TYPE (annual, perennial, vegetable, flower, etc.)

FORM   SEEDS   PLANTS

BARE-ROOT   CONTAINER   OTHER

SOURCE

DATE PURCHASED OR RECEIVED

COST

CONDITION

DATE PLANTED   FIRST GERMINATION

TRANSPLANTED

LOCATION PLANTED

PROJECTED MATURE SIZE: HEIGHT   SPREAD

BLOOMING/FRUITING PERIOD

COLOR/FORM/FOLIAGE NOTES

YIELD (FRUITS/VEGETABLES/HERBS)

HOW DID THIS PLANT PERFORM?

Planting Records

COMMON NAME

BOTANICAL NAME

CULTIVAR OR VARIETY

TYPE (annual, perennial, vegetable, flower, etc.)

FORM   SEEDS   PLANTS

BARE-ROOT   CONTAINER   OTHER

SOURCE

DATE PURCHASED OR RECEIVED

COST

CONDITION

DATE PLANTED   FIRST GERMINATION

TRANSPLANTED

LOCATION PLANTED

PROJECTED MATURE SIZE: HEIGHT   SPREAD

BLOOMING/FRUITING PERIOD

COLOR/FORM/FOLIAGE NOTES

YIELD (FRUITS/VEGETABLES/HERBS)

HOW DID THIS PLANT PERFORM?

COMMON NAME

BOTANICAL NAME

CULTIVAR OR VARIETY

TYPE (annual, perennial, vegetable, flower, etc.)

FORM   SEEDS   PLANTS

BARE-ROOT   CONTAINER   OTHER

SOURCE

DATE PURCHASED OR RECEIVED

COST

CONDITION

DATE PLANTED   FIRST GERMINATION

TRANSPLANTED

LOCATION PLANTED

PROJECTED MATURE SIZE: HEIGHT   SPREAD

BLOOMING/FRUITING PERIOD

COLOR/FORM/FOLIAGE NOTES

YIELD (FRUITS/VEGETABLES/HERBS)

HOW DID THIS PLANT PERFORM?

COMMON NAME

BOTANICAL NAME

CULTIVAR OR VARIETY

TYPE (annual, perennial, vegetable, flower, etc.)

FORM   SEEDS   PLANTS

BARE-ROOT   CONTAINER   OTHER

SOURCE

DATE PURCHASED OR RECEIVED

COST

CONDITION

DATE PLANTED   FIRST GERMINATION

TRANSPLANTED

LOCATION PLANTED

PROJECTED MATURE SIZE: HEIGHT   SPREAD

BLOOMING/FRUITING PERIOD

COLOR/FORM/FOLIAGE NOTES

YIELD (FRUITS/VEGETABLES/HERBS)

HOW DID THIS PLANT PERFORM?

COMMON NAME

BOTANICAL NAME

CULTIVAR OR VARIETY

TYPE (annual, perennial, vegetable, flower, etc.)

FORM   SEEDS   PLANTS

BARE-ROOT   CONTAINER   OTHER

SOURCE

DATE PURCHASED OR RECEIVED

COST

CONDITION

DATE PLANTED   FIRST GERMINATION

TRANSPLANTED

LOCATION PLANTED

PROJECTED MATURE SIZE: HEIGHT   SPREAD

BLOOMING/FRUITING PERIOD

COLOR/FORM/FOLIAGE NOTES

YIELD (FRUITS/VEGETABLES/HERBS)

HOW DID THIS PLANT PERFORM?

Planting Records

COMMON NAME

BOTANICAL NAME

CULTIVAR OR VARIETY

TYPE (annual, perennial, vegetable, flower, etc.)

FORM   SEEDS   PLANTS

BARE-ROOT   CONTAINER   OTHER

SOURCE

DATE PURCHASED OR RECEIVED

COST

CONDITION

DATE PLANTED   FIRST GERMINATION

TRANSPLANTED

LOCATION PLANTED

PROJECTED MATURE SIZE: HEIGHT   SPREAD

BLOOMING/FRUITING PERIOD

COLOR/FORM/FOLIAGE NOTES

YIELD (FRUITS/VEGETABLES/HERBS)

HOW DID THIS PLANT PERFORM?

COMMON NAME

BOTANICAL NAME

CULTIVAR OR VARIETY

TYPE (annual, perennial, vegetable, flower, etc.)

FORM   SEEDS   PLANTS

BARE-ROOT   CONTAINER   OTHER

SOURCE

DATE PURCHASED OR RECEIVED

COST

CONDITION

DATE PLANTED   FIRST GERMINATION

TRANSPLANTED

LOCATION PLANTED

PROJECTED MATURE SIZE: HEIGHT   SPREAD

BLOOMING/FRUITING PERIOD

COLOR/FORM/FOLIAGE NOTES

YIELD (FRUITS/VEGETABLES/HERBS)

HOW DID THIS PLANT PERFORM?

COMMON NAME

BOTANICAL NAME

CULTIVAR OR VARIETY

TYPE (annual, perennial, vegetable, flower, etc.)

FORM   SEEDS   PLANTS

BARE-ROOT   CONTAINER   OTHER

SOURCE

DATE PURCHASED OR RECEIVED

COST

CONDITION

DATE PLANTED   FIRST GERMINATION

TRANSPLANTED

LOCATION PLANTED

PROJECTED MATURE SIZE: HEIGHT   SPREAD

BLOOMING/FRUITING PERIOD

COLOR/FORM/FOLIAGE NOTES

YIELD (FRUITS/VEGETABLES/HERBS)

HOW DID THIS PLANT PERFORM?

COMMON NAME

BOTANICAL NAME

CULTIVAR OR VARIETY

TYPE (annual, perennial, vegetable, flower, etc.)

FORM   SEEDS   PLANTS

BARE-ROOT   CONTAINER   OTHER

SOURCE

DATE PURCHASED OR RECEIVED

COST

CONDITION

DATE PLANTED   FIRST GERMINATION

TRANSPLANTED

LOCATION PLANTED

PROJECTED MATURE SIZE: HEIGHT   SPREAD

BLOOMING/FRUITING PERIOD

COLOR/FORM/FOLIAGE NOTES

YIELD (FRUITS/VEGETABLES/HERBS)

HOW DID THIS PLANT PERFORM?

Planting Records

COMMON NAME

BOTANICAL NAME

CULTIVAR OR VARIETY

TYPE (annual, perennial, vegetable, flower, etc.)

FORM   SEEDS   PLANTS

BARE-ROOT   CONTAINER   OTHER

SOURCE

DATE PURCHASED OR RECEIVED

COST

CONDITION

DATE PLANTED   FIRST GERMINATION

TRANSPLANTED

LOCATION PLANTED

PROJECTED MATURE SIZE: HEIGHT   SPREAD

BLOOMING/FRUITING PERIOD

COLOR/FORM/FOLIAGE NOTES

YIELD (FRUITS/VEGETABLES/HERBS)

HOW DID THIS PLANT PERFORM?

COMMON NAME

BOTANICAL NAME

CULTIVAR OR VARIETY

TYPE (annual, perennial, vegetable, flower, etc.)

FORM   SEEDS   PLANTS

BARE-ROOT   CONTAINER   OTHER

SOURCE

DATE PURCHASED OR RECEIVED

COST

CONDITION

DATE PLANTED   FIRST GERMINATION

TRANSPLANTED

LOCATION PLANTED

PROJECTED MATURE SIZE: HEIGHT   SPREAD

BLOOMING/FRUITING PERIOD

COLOR/FORM/FOLIAGE NOTES

YIELD (FRUITS/VEGETABLES/HERBS)

HOW DID THIS PLANT PERFORM?

COMMON NAME

BOTANICAL NAME

CULTIVAR OR VARIETY

TYPE (annual, perennial, vegetable, flower, etc.)

FORM   SEEDS   PLANTS

BARE-ROOT   CONTAINER   OTHER

SOURCE

DATE PURCHASED OR RECEIVED

COST

CONDITION

DATE PLANTED   FIRST GERMINATION

TRANSPLANTED

LOCATION PLANTED

PROJECTED MATURE SIZE: HEIGHT   SPREAD

BLOOMING/FRUITING PERIOD

COLOR/FORM/FOLIAGE NOTES

YIELD (FRUITS/VEGETABLES/HERBS)

HOW DID THIS PLANT PERFORM?

COMMON NAME

BOTANICAL NAME

CULTIVAR OR VARIETY

TYPE (annual, perennial, vegetable, flower, etc.)

FORM   SEEDS   PLANTS

BARE-ROOT   CONTAINER   OTHER

SOURCE

DATE PURCHASED OR RECEIVED

COST

CONDITION

DATE PLANTED   FIRST GERMINATION

TRANSPLANTED

LOCATION PLANTED

PROJECTED MATURE SIZE: HEIGHT   SPREAD

BLOOMING/FRUITING PERIOD

COLOR/FORM/FOLIAGE NOTES

YIELD (FRUITS/VEGETABLES/HERBS)

HOW DID THIS PLANT PERFORM?

Planting Records

COMMON NAME

BOTANICAL NAME

CULTIVAR OR VARIETY

TYPE (annual, perennial, vegetable, flower, etc.)

FORM   SEEDS   PLANTS

BARE-ROOT   CONTAINER   OTHER

SOURCE

DATE PURCHASED OR RECEIVED

COST

CONDITION

DATE PLANTED   FIRST GERMINATION

TRANSPLANTED

LOCATION PLANTED

PROJECTED MATURE SIZE: HEIGHT   SPREAD

BLOOMING/FRUITING PERIOD

COLOR/FORM/FOLIAGE NOTES

YIELD (FRUITS/VEGETABLES/HERBS)

HOW DID THIS PLANT PERFORM?

COMMON NAME

BOTANICAL NAME

CULTIVAR OR VARIETY

TYPE (annual, perennial, vegetable, flower, etc.)

FORM   SEEDS   PLANTS

BARE-ROOT   CONTAINER   OTHER

SOURCE

DATE PURCHASED OR RECEIVED

COST

CONDITION

DATE PLANTED   FIRST GERMINATION

TRANSPLANTED

LOCATION PLANTED

PROJECTED MATURE SIZE: HEIGHT   SPREAD

BLOOMING/FRUITING PERIOD

COLOR/FORM/FOLIAGE NOTES

YIELD (FRUITS/VEGETABLES/HERBS)

HOW DID THIS PLANT PERFORM?

Sources: Plants, Seeds and Supplies

SEEDS

Burpee
300 Park Ave.
Warminster, PA 18974
800-333-5808
www.burpee.com

Cook's Garden
P.O. Box C5030
Warminster, PA 18974
800-457-9703
www.cooksgarden.com

Johnny's Selected Seeds
955 Benton Ave.
Winslow, ME 04901
877-564-6697
www.johnnyseeds.com

Nichols Garden Nursery
1190 Old Salem Rd. NE
Albany, OR 97321
800-422-3985
www.nicholsgardennursery.com

Park Seed
1 Parkton Ave.
Greenwood, SC 29647
800-213-0076
www.parkseed.com

PERENNIALS

Milaeger's Gardens
4838 Douglas Ave.
Racine, WI 53402
800-669-1229
www.milaegers.com

Niche Gardens
111 Dawson Road
Chapel Hill, NC 27516
919-967-0078
www.nichegardens.com

Siskiyou Rare Plant Nursery
2115 Talent Ave.
Talent, OR 97540
541-535-2113
www.siskiyourareplantnursery.com

Wayside Gardens
1 Garden Lane
Hodges, SC 26965
800-213-0379
www.waysidegardens.com

BULBS

Brent and Becky's Bulbs
7900 Daffodil Ln.
Gloucester, VA 23061
804-693-3966
www.brentandbeckysbulbs.com

McClure & Zimmerman
P.O. Box 368
Friesland, WI 53935
800-546-4053
www.mzbulb.com

Van Bourgondien
P.O. Box 2000
Virginia Beach, VA 23450
800-622-9997
www.dutchbulbs.com

SUPPLIES

Gardener's Supply Co.
128 Intervale Road
Burlington, VT 05041
800-833-1412
www.gardeners.com

Gardens Alive!
5100 Schenley Place
Lawrenceburg, IN 47025
513-354-1482
www.gardensalive.com

Peaceful Valley Farm Supply
P.O. Box 2209
Grass Valley, CA 95945
888-784-1722
www.groworganic.com

Your well-used gardening catalogs rest next to your couch. The nursery's number is on a dog-eared page in the phonebook. The county extension office's number is on that pamphlet in the "junk drawer." Wouldn't it be nice to have one central location for all your gardening resources and contact information? Here it is! All you have to do is take a few minutes to write everything down now ... and save yourself tons of time later.

My favorite resources and local nurseries:

NAME

ADDRESS

PHONE   WEB SITE

NOTES

NAME

ADDRESS

PHONE   WEB SITE

NOTES

NAME

ADDRESS

PHONE   WEB SITE

NOTES

Great Gardens to Visit

Botanical gardens offer us a place to see how the pros design and grow their gardens. You often see new plant introductions before they're ready for the public market. Botanical gardens also put on terrific programs and fun events. Here's a place to keep track of botanical gardens, arboreta, display gardens or favorite home gardens in your area, or in places you plan to travel to.

GARDEN

ADDRESS

PHONE
WEB SITE
NOTES

GARDEN

ADDRESS

PHONE
WEB SITE
NOTES

GARDEN

ADDRESS

PHONE
WEB SITE
NOTES

GARDEN

ADDRESS

PHONE
WEB SITE
NOTES

GARDEN

ADDRESS

PHONE
WEB SITE
NOTES

Local Clubs and Gardening Organizations

Here's a handy place to record "vitals" on local clubs, organizations and other gardening resources.

NAME

ADDRESS

PHONE   WEB SITE

NOTES

NAME

ADDRESS

PHONE   WEB SITE

NOTES

NAME

ADDRESS

PHONE   WEB SITE

NOTES

National Home Gardening Club web site: www.gardeningclub.com

NAME

ADDRESS

PHONE   WEB SITE

NOTES

NAME

ADDRESS

PHONE   WEB SITE

NOTES

NAME

ADDRESS

PHONE   WEB SITE

NOTES

MASTER GARDENER HOTLINES

PHONE

PHONE

Plant Societies

Plant and gardening societies offer gardeners an opportunity to learn more about gardening in general and specific plants in detail, both from publications and from spending time with other gardeners.

The American Dianthus Society
P. O. Box 188
Pegram, TN 37143
615-353-1092

American Fern Society
456 McGill Place
Atlanta, GA 30312
www.amerfersoc.com

American Hemerocallis Society
1454 Rebel Drive
Jackson, MS 39211
www.daylilies.com

American Horticultural Society
Alexandria, VA 22308-1300
www.ahs.org

American Hosta Society
7802 NE 63rd Street
Vancouver, WA 98662
giboshiman@aol.com
www.americanhostasociety.com

American Iris Society
P. O. Box 177
DeLeon Springs, FL 32130
www.irises.org

Sections of AIS include:
   Dwarf Iris Society of America
   Historic Iris Preservation Society
   Louisiana Iris Society of America
   The Reblooming Iris Society
   The Society for Japanese Irises

Society for Pacific Native Iris
Society for Siberian Irises
Species Iris Group of North America
Spuria Iris Society

American Penstemon Society
1050 Camino Rancheros
Santa Fe, NM 87505
www.apsdev.org

American Peony Society
250 Interlachen Road
Hopkins, MN 55343
www.americanpeonysociety.org

American Primrose, Primula & Auricula Society
9705 SE Spring Crest Drive
Portland, OR 97225
www.americanprimrosesociety.org

American Rock Garden Society
P. O. Box 67
Millwood, NY 10546
www.nargs.com

Cottage Garden Society
5 Nixon Close, Thornhill
Dewsbury, West Yorkshire
England WR12 OJA
www.thecgs.org.uk

The Flower and Herb Exchange
3094 North Winn Road
Decorah, IA 52101
www.seedsavers.org

Hardy Fern Foundation
P. O. Box 3797
Federal City, WA 98063
www.hardyferns.org

The Hardy Plant Society
Little Orchard, Great Comberton
Pershore, Worcestershire
England WR10 3DP
www.hardy-plant.org.uk

Hardy Plant Society of Oregon
1930 NW Lovejoy St.
Portland, OR 97209
www.hardyplantsociety.org

International Violet Association
8604 Main Road
Berlin Heights, OH 44814-9620
www.americanvioletsociety.org

Los Angeles International Fern Society
P. O. Box 90943
Pasadena, CA 91109-0943
www.iaifs.org

National Chrysanthemum Society
10107 Homar Pond Drive
Fairfax Station, VA 22039-1650
www.mums.org

Northwest Perennial Alliance
8522 46th St. NW
Gig Harbor, WA 98335
www.northwestperennialalliance.org

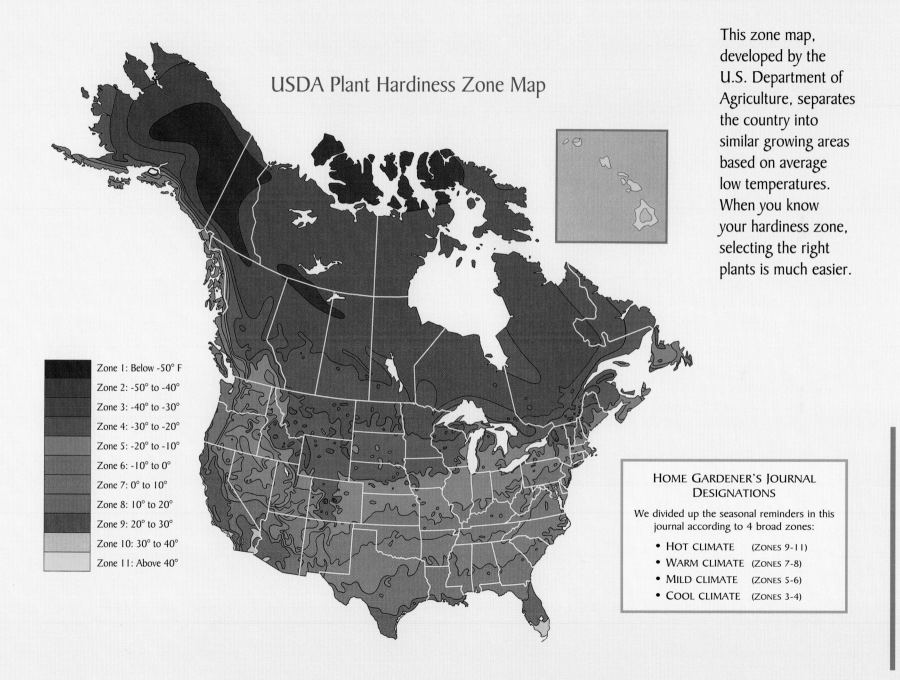

USDA Plant Hardiness Zone Map

This zone map, developed by the U.S. Department of Agriculture, separates the country into similar growing areas based on average low temperatures. When you know your hardiness zone, selecting the right plants is much easier.

Zone 1: Below -50° F
Zone 2: -50° to -40°
Zone 3: -40° to -30°
Zone 4: -30° to -20°
Zone 5: -20° to -10°
Zone 6: -10° to 0°
Zone 7: 0° to 10°
Zone 8: 10° to 20°
Zone 9: 20° to 30°
Zone 10: 30° to 40°
Zone 11: Above 40°

HOME GARDENER'S JOURNAL DESIGNATIONS

We divided up the seasonal reminders in this journal according to 4 broad zones:

- HOT CLIMATE   (ZONES 9-11)
- WARM CLIMATE   (ZONES 7-8)
- MILD CLIMATE   (ZONES 5-6)
- COOL CLIMATE   (ZONES 3-4)

References

	June
	May
	April
	March
	February
	January

Average Dates of Last Spring Frost

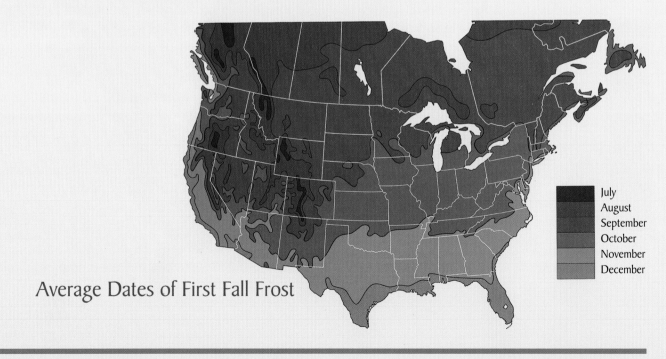

	July
	August
	September
	October
	November
	December

Average Dates of First Fall Frost

acid soil n. Soil with a pH of less than 7.0. Most plants do best in soils with a pH of 6.5 to 6.8. Also called "sour" soil. See pH factor.

aerate v. To alter soil texture and structure by creating more air spaces, often by spiking.

alba adj. Latin for white.

alkaline soil n. Soil with a pH of 7.1 or higher. Also called "sweet" or "basic" soil. See pH factor.

arch n. A supporting structure for climbing vines or upright plants that forms an opening or passageway.

bare-root plant n. One bought or shipped without soil.

bower n. An arch-shaped trellis, usually with latticework, for supporting plants.

bud n. A swelling that contains undeveloped or unopened leaves or flowers.

budding n. A propagation method of grafting a leaf bud onto rootstock.

bud union n. The part of a grafted plant where the understock meets the bud, out of which forms the top growth, a swollen "knob" generally a few inches above the roots.

bulb n. A group of swollen, modified, underground leaves that act as a storage organ.

bush n. A small or neatly trained shrub.

calyx n. The green cover of the flower bud, formed from the sepals, which protects the bud.

cane n. A basal shoot or main stem.

compost n. Material rich in nutrients, the result of decomposed organic matter. Used as a soil amendment or mulch. v. To convert something to compost.

crown n. The area where the canes or stems sprout from the bud union.

cultivar n. A contraction of "cultivated variety" of a plant. Abbr.: cv. Cultivars retain their characteristics when propagated.

deadhead v. To remove flower heads or spent flowers.

deciduous adj. Losing leaves every year in autumn and winter.

dieback n. The dying of plant tips or shoots from climate or disease.

disbud v. To remove buds to promote production of larger or better-quality blooms.

division n. A propagation method that involves dividing a plant into separate parts.

dormant adj. A plant that has temporarily stopped growth, usually in winter.

evergreen adj. Retaining leaves throughout the year.

family n. A group of related genera. Daisies are of the family *Compositae*.

flush n. A bloom period.

genus (pl. genera) n. A group of plants with common characteristics. Designated with italics and a capital letter: *Tulipa* is the genus of the tulips.

graft union n. The point where top growth has been grafted onto the rootstock.

grafting n. A propagation method where one plant is created by uniting a shoot or bud with a rootstock of two different plants.

groundcover n., adj. A low-growing plant; often one that spreads well.

harden off v. To acclimate a young plant raised in a protected environment to cooler conditions.

hardiness n. The ability of a plant to survive freezing temperatures outside. See zone.

hardpan n. A subsoil layer so compacted that it impedes or prevents root penetration.

hardy adj. Able to withstand frost and cold and therefore grow outside throughout the year.

heat-zone system n. A rating based on the number of days with temperatures over 86° F, when heat stress begins to affect plants.

heel in v. To plant in a temporary location.

hip n. The fruit of the rose, a seedpod that turns shades of red when ripe. Many roses' hips are high in vitamin C and are eaten by birds and, in some forms, by people.

hybrid n. The result of a cross between two different species or varieties.

lateral cane n. A side branch of a main cane.

leaf node n. The point where a cane or stem bears a leaf bud or leaf.

lutea adj. Latin for yellow.

neutral soil n. Soil with a pH of 7.0. See pH factor.

non-remontant adj. Blooming once in a growing season.

own-root adj. Grown from cuttings; a plant not budded onto another stock.

Glossary

patented adj. Varieties or cultivars protected by government patent. U.S. plant patents last for 17 years and serve to guarantee that the plant you buy is true to name.

perennial n, adj. A plant that lives in outdoor conditions for more than two years.

pergola n. A structure of pillars and crosspieces used to create a walkway covered by trained plants.

perpetual-flowering adj. Synonym of remontant.

petal n. The showy part of the flower within the sepals.

pH factor n. A measure of a soil's acidity or alkalinity based on hydrogen ions. See also acidic soil, alkaline soil, neutral soil.

PPAF adj. Plant Patent Applied For, an official designation of U.S. patent status.

prickle n. Officially, the sharp protective points on a plant. "Thorn" is a more commonly used term.

pruning n. Selectively cutting a plant for better health, production, and/or shape.

quartered adj. A petal form where the center petals are folded into four quarters. One example is the rose 'Souvenir de la Malmaison'.

recurrent adj. Synonym of repeat-flowering.

remontant adj. Flowering more than once during a growing season, whether continually or intermittently.

repeat-flowering adj. Flowering again after the first or main blooming flush.

rhizome n. A swollen stem that grows horizontally, producing roots and shoots.

rootstock n. The understock or host plant used for grafting a bud or scion.

Rosaceae n. A large family, containing over 100 genera (including those of cherries, plums, pears, apples, hawthorns and serviceberries) and 3,000 species.

rugose adj. Wrinkled, as the leaves of *Rosa rugosa*.

scion n. A bud or shoot used in grafting to a rootstock.

sepal n. Part of the protective calyx surrounding the petals, sometimes showy.

shoot n. A stem or cane.

shrub n, adj. 1) A class of versatile, tough roses that can be used for hedges, groundcovers, mixed with others in borders, etc. 2) Any plant with woody and multiple stems.

species n. Plants that share distinctive essential features—leaf shape, flower color—and breed true. Species serve several gardening purposes besides providing vital breeding stock.

specimen plant n. One grown or placed to accent its features as an individual plant, as opposed to its role in a group.

sport n. A natural change in a plant's genetic makeup, for example, a bush-form plant that suddenly becomes a climber.

standard n. Any plant trained and shaped to grow on one trunk.

stock: n. see rootstock.

sucker n. A stem or shoot that rises from rootstock below the bud union.

tender adj. Injured or killed by cold weather and frost.

thorn n. A sharp spine or prickle on a stem that protects the plant from predators (and reminds the gardener to be careful).

tilth n. General condition or quality of a soil, used for soil as "health" is used for living organisms.

understock n. The plant that gives the rootstock for grafting.

variety n. (abbr.: var.) Generally, any distinct form of a species or hybrid. Technically, a variant of a species in the wild that breeds true. See cultivar.

winterize v. To protect from the cold.

winter-kill n. Death of plant cells or plants due to winter conditions.

zone n. A designation for an area with similar hardiness conditions. Perennials are rated by a system of hardiness zones; for example, a Zone 4 plant will tolerate ,